A Day at CHÂTEAU DE FONTAINEBLEAU

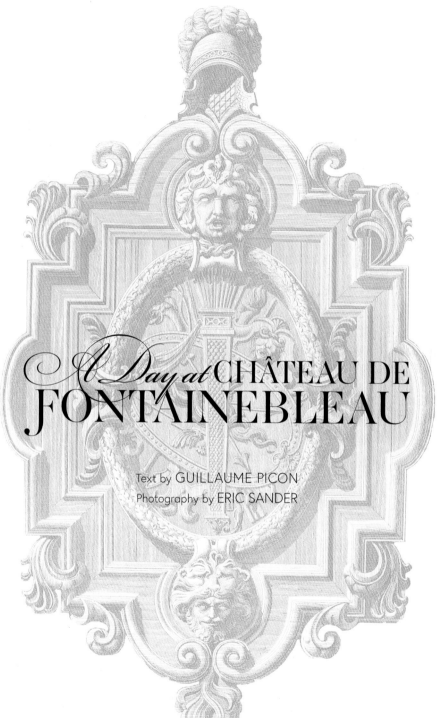

A Day at CHÂTEAU DE FONTAINEBLEAU

Text by GUILLAUME PICON

Photography by ERIC SANDER

Château
de Fontainebleau

Flammarion

Contents

PAGES 2–3
Door to the François I Gallery, carved by Jean Gobert in 1639.

PAGES 4–5
*View of the Château and Gardens at Fontainebleau after
the Improvements of 1713*, by Pierre Denis Martin: a faithful depiction
of the royal residence at the end of Louis XIV's reign.

FACING PAGE
Detail of the celebrated horseshoe-shaped staircase built during
the reign of Louis XIII. Engraving from the *Monographie du Palais de
Fontainebleau*, drawn and engraved by Rodolphe Pfnor.

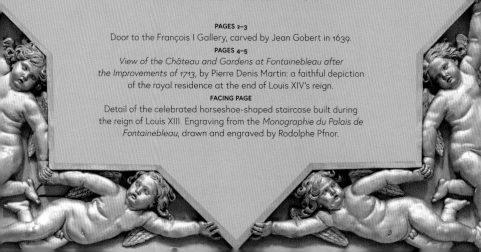

Foreword

A château with "the shape and color of time." Such lyricism may come as something of a surprise from Napoléon, but these were the poetic terms he chose to describe Fontainebleau. This was the palace that he preferred to Versailles, which he found too grandiloquent, too much the vision of one man. The palace whose very lack of symmetry and uniformity—the legacy of its centuries of history—he loved. The palace that he was to view as the "true residence of kings," and on which virtually all of those sovereigns had left their mark.

When Napoléon first visited Fontainebleau, in 1803, the château was a mere shadow of its former self. The Revolution had emptied it of its furniture, which had been sold off in the Cour de la Fontaine (Fountain Courtyard). The tapestries that had hung on the walls, the crystal chandeliers, the precious mirrors—all were gone. Through the gaping windows, most of them now with their frames torn out, the wind gusted down the empty passages of a deserted palace. A training academy for army officers had taken over the buildings on the Cour du Cheval Blanc (White Horse Courtyard). The Carp Pond had become a swimming pool for the cadets.

But the majestic decorative schemes that been the glory of Fontainebleau remained in situ, and the palace walls still held memories of the splendors of the French court. When Napoléon sought a fitting place in which to receive Pope Pius VII, who was to anoint him at his coronation in Notre Dame on December 2, 1804, he looked no further than this palace that had welcomed a succession of prestigious guests since the reign of François I. Fontaine and Duroc, the palace architect and grand marshal respectively, were given orders to make all the preparations necessary for Fontainebleau to house the pontiff. Just nineteen days later, all was in place: forty principal apartments, two hundred lodgings for the papal retinue, and stables for four hundred horses lay in readiness for the emperor's guests. To achieve this feat, Fontaine and Duroc had brought out old furniture from the stores of the Garde-Meuble de la Couronne (Royal Furniture Warehouse), now the Mobilier Impérial; they had bought new furniture to fill any gaps; and they had commissioned new pieces from cabinetmakers'

workshops. When they ran out of transport vehicles, Duroc drafted in gun carriages to convey the furniture from Paris. On the arrival of the papal retinue, Napoléon went out to meet the pontiff at a lavish ceremony in a clearing in the forest of Fontainebleau.

Eight years later, the pope was back at Fontainebleau; this time, however, he was a high-security prisoner. In the intervening years, relations between the papacy and the emperor had soured, and in 1808 Rome had been occupied by Napoleonic troops. The following year, the pope was arrested and detained successively at Grenoble, Valence, Avignon, and Savona in Liguria. On May 21, 1812, Napoléon ordered his return to France, and on April 19 he arrived at Fontainebleau.

Pius VII's eighteen-month captivity must have allowed him ample leisure to admire the palace decorations. He might almost have been reminded of his Italian home, for in the years from 1530 to 1570 Fontainebleau had welcomed a galaxy of Italian artists. In his *Lives of the Most Eminent Painters, Sculptors and Architects*, Vasari even described Fontainebleau under the Valois kings as a "new Rome." The Galerie François I (François I Gallery), Renaissance masterpiece and manifesto of the first Fontainebleau School, served as the pope's exercise yard. Did he tease out the secrets of the Rosso Fiorentino frescoes, in their frames of exuberantly sensual stucco work? Was he moved by the chilly charms of the large female nudes with which Primaticcio had decked the bedchamber of the king's mistress, the Duchesse d'Étampes? And what did he make of the profusion of mythological scenes with which Niccolò dell'Abate had covered the walls, pillars and spandrels of the Ballroom, completed under Henri II? Of one thing we may be certain: for Pius VII, Fontainebleau was a solitary and melancholy place where he measured out the many layers of time.

This is the palace into which this book invites the visitors of today, in their turn. Nearly a thousand years have shaped this residence of French kings and emperors of every dynasty—Capetian, Valois, Bourbon, Bonaparte, and Orléans. United by their passion for the sport of kings and the teeming game to be found in its magnificent forests, they have bequeathed Fontainebleau to succeeding generations. Down the centuries, every passing era has left its mark on the fabric of this remarkable palace.

The form and color—and the layers—of time.

JEAN-FRANÇOIS HEBERT
President of the château de Fontainebleau

FACING PAGE
Rising at the far end of the White Horse Courtyard, the horseshoe-shaped staircase is an iconic feature of the palace of Fontainebleau. It has formed the main entrance to the château since Napoléon Bonaparte opened up the courtyard by constructing imposing gates.

PAGES 12–13
The Porte Dauphine, the monumental gateway built at the eastern extremity of the Oval Courtyard under Henri IV. Detail of an engraving after a drawing by Israël Silvestre, seventeenth century.

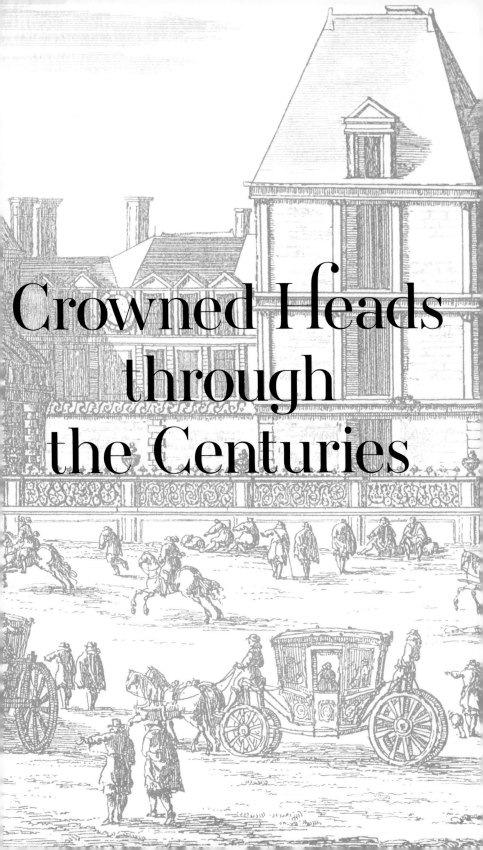

Crowned Heads through the Centuries

The Medieval Castle

It was in 1137 that Fontainebleau—in the words of Jean Vatout, a poet and historian who was close to Louis-Philippe, king of the French from 1830 to 1848—"made its sudden entrance into the annals of history." It was in that year, with little fanfare, that Louis VII signed a charter confirming the foundation of an abbey at Fontainebleau in the Val d'Oise. There have been more dramatic entrances into history, but this document nevertheless contains one of the earliest known references to Fontainebleau. The year 1137 was also marked by momentous events. In July, Louis VII married Eleanor, heiress to the duchy of Aquitaine and the county of Poitiers. A few days later, he succeeded his father Louis VI ("the Fat") on the throne, and as the newly crowned king bestowed his favor and that of his entourage on Fontainebleau.

Little is known about the appearance of the castle at this period. The keep that we see today already stood, and was probably protected by a defensive wall flanked by towers and ringed by a ditch. The years went by, and in 1169 a new chapel was consecrated within the castle walls. It was dedicated to Saint Saturnin—now largely forgotten but at that time celebrated as one of the martyrs of Christian Gaul—in a ceremony presided over by Thomas Becket, Archbishop of Canterbury, former chancellor to the English king Henry II, and highly distinguished figure who had fled to France in the wake of his dispute with Henry. This protection offered by Louis VII to an adversary of the English king should be viewed in the context of the hostility that had reigned between the Capetian and Plantagenet kings for over a decade.

When Philippe-Auguste acceded to the throne in 1180, he was mindful of his father's attachment to Fontainebleau and made a generous endowment of alms to the Saint-Saturnin Chapel. His grandson Louis IX, the future Saint Louis, embarked on building works that are commemorated

FACING PAGE
The ground floor of the medieval keep, transformed under Louis-Philippe into a Gothic-style vestibule known as the Vestibule Saint-Louis.

PAGE 16
The Vestibule Saint-Louis is decorated with plaster statues of the French kings, here Philippe-Auguste.

today in the two rooms that bear his name on the first floor of the old castle. Louis IX's relationship with Fontainebleau focused largely on the monastery hospital that he founded there in 1259, under the direction of monks of the Trinitarian order. The last kings of the Capetian dynasty also spent time at Fontainebleau, as did the Valois who came after them. In a letter written in 1431, Charles VII, known disparagingly as the "King of Bourges" and battling to regain his kingdom from the English and the dukes of Burgundy, described the works undertaken at Fontainebleau by his mother, Isabeau of Bavaria. The air in this pleasant spot was believed to be beneficial and to have health-giving properties. Had the royal family itself not sought refuge there when the plague swept Europe in 1348? With the exception of the enlargements carried out by Isabeau, vestiges of which can still be seen here and there in the façades overlooking the Cour Ovale (Oval Courtyard), the Valois did not display any particular fondness for Fontainebleau in the fifteenth century. Charles VIII and Louis XII preferred instead to embellish the Loire châteaux with masterpieces brought back from Italy. It would fall to François I to transform Fontainebleau into a palace fit for a Renaissance prince.

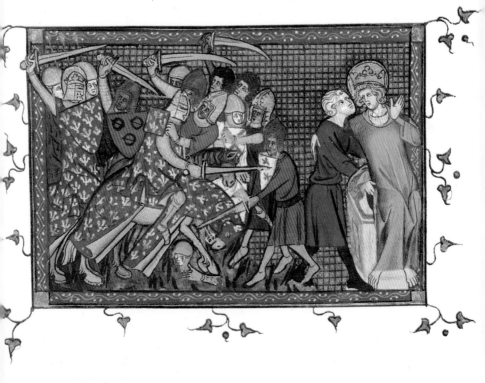

Fontainebleau:
"Cultural Capital of the Kingdom"

On January 1, 1515, Louis XII died, and his cousin François d'Angoulême acceded to the throne as François I.
On September 13–14 that same year, François won a victory at the Battle of Marignano in northern Italy, which enabled him to consolidate his dominance over the Duchy of Milan. Apart from this military success—soon to be tempered by defeats on other battlefields—François's contemporaries and his modern biographers alike are unanimous in highlighting one aspect of his reign: his support and development of the arts, as both king and patron, which raised them to new and unprecedented heights in France.

Among the many and varied forms of art in which François took an interest, he displayed a particular passion for architecture. During his first decade on the throne, he commissioned major building works at some of the royal châteaux in the Loire Valley, including Amboise, where he had spent part of his childhood; Blois, his predecessor's favorite residence; and Chambord, which he built from 1519. From the mid-1520s, however, he forsook the Loire Valley and turned instead to his châteaux in the Île-de-France, including the most prominent among them: Fontainebleau. The château he had inherited from the Capetian kings proved too small to accommodate François I and his court, however, and in 1528, he decided on a number of building projects with a view to enlarging it. The first of these concerned the medieval château, which he largely remodeled while at the same time retaining its layout around the oval courtyard. Evidence of this building campaign may be seen in the Porte Dorée (Golden Gate) that replaced the gateway to the old fortress, complete with its loggias inspired by the Palazzo Ducale in Urbino. His next move was to acquire the monastery founded by Louis VII, and to use the extra space thus gained to lay out a vast courtyard known as the Cour du Cheval blanc (White Horse Courtyard). Soon this was lined with four low

'The king brought me to his gallery, the key of which he keeps on his person.... After that I had well beheld the said gallery me thought it the most magnifique that ever I saw. [The gallery is paneled all around and] betwixt every window stands great anticall [antique] personages entier [full-length]. And in diverse places of the said gallery many fair tables [paintings] of stories set in very finely wrought.

SIR JOHN WALLOP, ROYAL ENVOY, IN A LETTER TO HENRY VIII, 1540

FACING PAGE

Detail of the *Royal Elephant*, one of the frescoes in the François I Gallery. Wearing a shield bearing a salamander on its forehead, the white elephant is an allegorical portrait of François I. This image falls within a long tradition stretching back to antiquity of depicting elephants as symbols of wisdom and royalty.

PAGES 30–31

Detail from *The Unity of the State* tapestry, depicting François I holding a pomegranate, symbol of unity. François I commanded that six tapestries reprising frescoes by Rosso Fiorentino and their stucco decoration should be woven at Fontainebleau.

rectilinear wings punctuated with square or rectangular pavilions. Replacing as they did the classic round towers of medieval castle architecture, these represented an important new development in architecture. The east wing included the monastery chapel, linked to the old château by a gallery. François continued to make improvements and carry out new building projects right up to the end of his reign. In the White Horse Courtyard, the south wing was simultaneously raised and extended to create a gallery; and in 1541 work started on the building of a new chapel on two levels in the old château, which was to take fifteen years to complete.

Fontainebleau also owed its success to the peerless quality of its interior decorations. François I took advantage of his various military campaigns in Italy to invite a number of Italian artists to France. In 1531, he summoned Rosso Fiorentino to his service, and entrusted him with the decoration of the château interiors. Rosso's unchallenged masterpiece remains the Grande Galerie or Galerie François I (Great Gallery or François I Gallery), linking the east wing of the White Horse Courtyard and the royal apartments in the medieval keep. Rosso was not the only artist to work on this gallery, but he was in overall charge of the work. The lower part of the walls is embellished with finely carved paneling by Scibec da Carpi featuring the "F" of the royal monogram with the king's emblem, the salamander. The originality of the decorations on the walls above the paneling lies in their astonishing combination of frescoes and the stucco carvings in high relief that frame them. Rosso's frescoes are distinguished by the originality of their Michelangelo-influenced Florentine Mannerist style, with a lively and clearly defined palette and a cleverly conceived iconography of allegories and symbols celebrating François I and the monarchy. A year after inviting Rosso to Fontainebleau, the king summoned Primaticcio to France. Arriving at Fontainebleau in 1532, Primaticcio worked under Rosso initially, before taking over the direction of the decorative works there on the older artist's death in 1540. With the other Italian, Flemish and French artists who worked alongside them, Rosso and Primaticcio were together responsible for the creation of the School of Fontainebleau, which through the medium of engravings was soon to become known throughout Europe. François I's wish that France should become an influential center of art was coming to pass. In the meantime, Fontainebleau became celebrated as the "cultural capital of the kingdom."

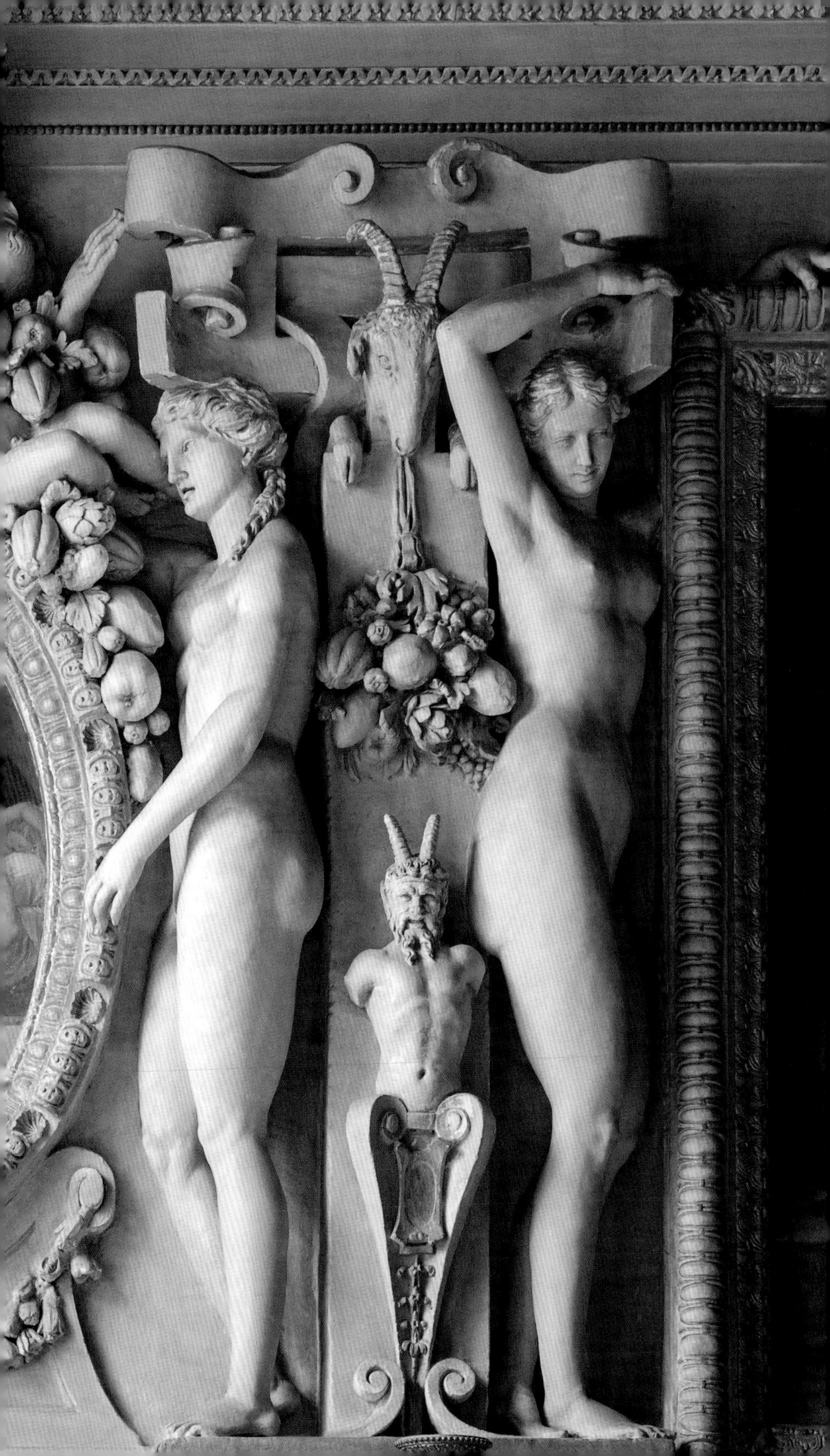

Henri II and His Sons

On March 31, 1547, François I's second son came to the throne as Henri II. Twenty-eight years of age, Henri had received an excellent education and was well versed in the arts. What was more, the new king soon proved to be a great builder. The Louvre was the first major building project of his reign, but it was not the only one, for he also turned his attention to Fontainebleau. The architect Philibert Delorme now took over as master of works, so allowing Primaticcio to focus on the château's interior decorations from conception to completion. At the end of François I's reign, work had begun on a building topped by a loggia and standing between the Golden Gate and the Saint-Saturnin Chapel. Now the plans were altered, and the loggia became the Salle de Bal (Ballroom), by which name it is still known today. Its painted decorations were by the Italian artist Niccolò dell'Abate, who had arrived in France from his native Modena in 1552. On the side of the courtyard that stood on the perimeter of the former monastery buildings, Delorme erected a monumental stair distinguished by its horseshoe shape.

Henri II's untimely death in 1559, when he was mortally wounded in a tournament held for the marriage of his daughter Élisabeth to Philip II of Spain, was to have repercussions for the building works then in progress at Fontainebleau. Following François II's short-lived reign in 1559–60, the accession of Charles IX (1560–74), who was still a minor, elevated Henri II's widow Catherine de' Medici to prominence as his regent. Catherine dismissed Delorme and promoted Primaticcio, appointing him superintendent of the royal buildings. He was to reign as master of works at Fontainebleau until his death in 1570. Between 1565 and 1570, he added a wing to the Cour de la Fontaine (Fountain Courtyard) with its entrance at first-floor level, reached by a great external stair of two symmetrical flights. His use of ashlar (dressed stone) masonry instead of the rubble masonry (coursed rows of sandstone, rubble and brick) employed under François I marked, according to Jean-Pierre Samoyault, a "revolution in château architecture." Primaticcio also erected the plaster statue of a horse—after the equestrian statue of Marcus Aurelius in Rome—from which the courtyard was to take its name.

FACING PAGE
The Ballroom was originally designed as an open loggia. Drawing by François Debret, nineteenth century.

PAGES 44–45
Begun under François I, the loggia was converted into a ballroom by Henri II. The frescoes were painted between 1550 and 1558 by Niccolò dell'Abate and his team, after drawings by Primaticcio.

•They were dazzled by the magnificence of the ceiling, which was divided into octagonal coffers highlighted in gold and silver, more finely chiselled than a jewel, and by the vast number of paintings that covered the walls, from the immense chimneypiece, where the arms of France were flanked by crescents and quivers, down to the musicians' gallery, which ran the full width of the other end of the hall.

GUSTAVE FLAUBERT, *A SENTIMENTAL EDUCATION*, 1869

FACING PAGE
The floor, paneling, and ceiling of the Ballroom were created by the cabinetmaker
Francesco Scibec da Carpi, who had already worked on the François I Gallery.
PAGES 48–49
A romanticized early nineteenth-century view of the Ballroom by Robit.
In fact the frescoes required restoration work as early as the reign of Henri IV.
This was not carried out until the nineteenth century, when the cycle
of frescoes was completed and repainted on the initiative of Louis-Philippe.
A new floor echoing the coffered ceiling was also laid.

The inscription on the lintel reads:

IMPERIO, NATISQVE POTENS ET CONIVGE FELIX,
ALTA PACE SACRAM DECORAT REX INCLITVS ÆDEM.
ÆTERNVM VT PIETAS AVGVSTA SPLENDEAT AVLA

1608   1608

ABOVE, FACING PAGE, AND PAGES 52–53
The organ tribune and doors to the upper chapel of Saint-Saturnin
date from the reign of Henri II, while the decorations of the walls and ceiling
were carried out under Henri IV. The upper chapel was converted
into a library under Napoléon Bonaparte; Napoléon III subsequently
moved the books into the Diana Gallery.

A cultivation of the arts was not sufficient for the safe governance of the kingdom, however, as emerged with great clarity in 1562. In that fateful year, tensions between Catholics and Protestants erupted into violent conflict, marking the beginning of the murderous Wars of Religion that were to rage—with interludes of fragile peace—for over thirty years. In 1565, against the background of this violent civil unrest in which the authority of the Crown was steadily eroded by the powerful nobles of the kingdom, Catherine de' Medici commanded Primaticcio to excavate a defensive ditch around the château. This was no time for embarking on any further additions to the château, and from being a brilliant center of new developments in architecture and the arts under François I and Henri II, Fontainebleau now fell into a period of semi-stagnation. In 1574, Charles IX's brother succeeded him as Henri III. Fifteen years later, the young king was assassinated by a fanatical Dominican friar by the name of Jacques Clément. As the last scion of the Valois dynasty, Henri III had designated the Bourbon Henri of Navarre as his successor. The Protestant Henri IV struggled to impose royal authority over his largely Catholic kingdom. Although he visited Fontainebleau from 1593, this was not the moment for new construction projects, or even for carrying out maintenance works on the royal châteaux in France and Navarre—let alone Spain, since the French who were hostile to Henri had appealed to the Spanish for their support.

ABOVE AND FACING PAGE
Nineteenth-century photograph of the Fine Fireplace Wing, and *Façade Overlooking
the Fountain Courtyard* by Jacques Androuet du Cerceau, 1579.
Built under Charles IX, the Fine Fireplace Wing is considered one of the great
masterpieces of French Renaissance architecture, representing a magnificent
synthesis of the governing principles of architecture in France and Italy in this period.
In less abstract terms, the rhythms of the pilasters and niches that enliven
the façade and the divergent double-flight staircase earn it an unchallenged place
among the "most excellent buildings of France", to borrow from the title of Androuet
du Cerceau's famous book (*Les plus excellents bâtiments de France*).

ONTAINEBLEAV

Face dans la court de la for...
Facies in aream spectans in q...
est fons

One of the most excellent
buildings of France.

JACQUES ANDROUET DU CERCEAU, 1579

Fontainebleau and the
House of ·Bourbon

BELOW, LEFT
The monogram of Henri IV
on a windowpane
in the Stags Gallery.
BELOW, RIGHT
Detail of one of the doors
leading into the second
Salle Saint-Louis.
FACING PAGE
Initially the King's
Bedchamber in the
sixteenth century and
subsequently the King's
Antechamber under the
Bourbons, the second
Salle Saint-Louis contains
the famous bas-relief
of Henri IV on horseback
by Mathieu Jacquet.
The figure was designed to
embellish the magnificent
fireplace that earned the
"Aile de la Belle Cheminée"
(Fine Fireplace Wing)
its name.

A bold military leader and shrewd politician, Henri IV realized that his victories on the field of battle were not sufficient in themselves to unite the kingdom around his person. His Protestant faith remained an insurmountable stumbling block in the eyes of his Catholic subjects. And if he had no choice but to convert if he wanted to secure his hold on the French throne, then—in the immortal words of his loyal companion in arms Sully—"Paris was well worth a Mass." His conversion to the Catholic faith, celebrated at Saint-Denis in July 1593, paved the way for his coronation; this was held the following February in Chartres Cathedral, rather than Reims as was the custom, since Reims lay in the hands of his enemies. Henri's conversion gained him the allegiance of the great majority of his subjects, and he was at last able to negotiate the surrender of Paris. On March 22, 1594, Henri IV made his entrance into his capital. His victory became complete in 1598, when he issued the Edict of Nantes, imposing religious tolerance on Catholics and Protestants alike. Henri IV was at last master of his kingdom.

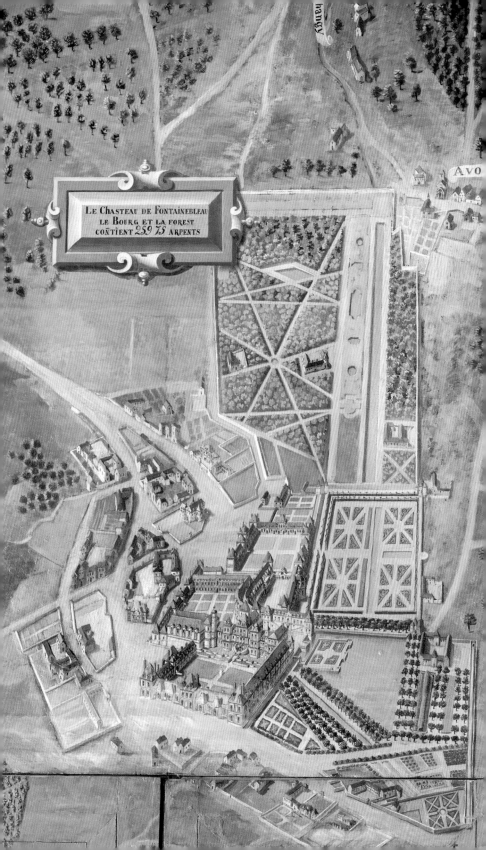

Le Chasteau de Fontainebleau
Le Bourg et la Forest
contient 25975 arpents

AVO

hangy

Constructed under Henri IV, the Stags Gallery is 243 feet long (74 meters) and 23 feet wide
(7 meters), and is decorated with views of the royal residences and game forests, interspersed
on the garden side with mounted stags' heads. Converted into additional apartments
for members of the royal family in the eighteenth century, it was restored
in the nineteenth century on the orders of Napoléon III.

PAGE 61
The Diana Fountain, installed in the Diana Garden under Henri IV.

FACING PAGE
A view of the palace of Fontainebleau painted at one end of the Stags Gallery.

ABOVE
The entrance to the Stags Gallery, showing the reverse of the figure
of the *Arrotino* ("blade sharpener") or *Scythian*, an eighteenth-century bronze
copy of a Greek statue of the third century BCE.

Our great king Henri IV has since decorated and enriched this residence a hundred times better, so that it is now changed beyond recognition from its former state. And this is not all; in the village that the king desired to wall around as a town, there stand some thirty houses, but what houses! Rather we should say thirty palaces, built ceaselessly by princes, cardinals and great lords in order to please their king…, in short, a little paradise in France!

PIERRE DE BOURDEILLE, *MÉMOIRES: VIES DES HOMMES ILLUSTRES ET DES GRANDS CAPITAINES*, 1665

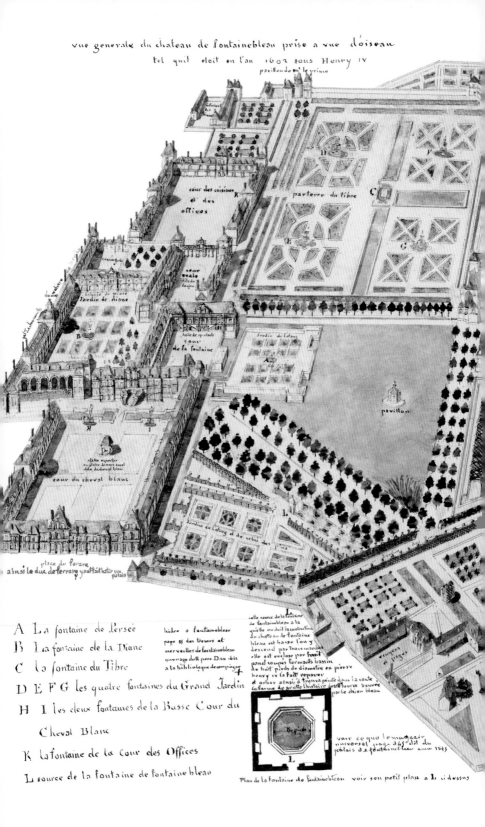

vue generale du chateau de fontainebleau prise a vue d'oiseau
tel quil eloit en l'an 1602 sous Henry IV
pavillon dont le prince

cour des cuisines
et des
offices

parterre du Tibre

cour
ovale
dite de
logis

Jardin de diane

Salle de spectacle
cour de la fontaine

Jardin du Letang

pavillon

cour du cheval blanc

place du Perare
ainsi le duc de ferrare y avait habiter un palais

Jardin du Letang et de celuis des Pins

A La fontaine de Persée
B La fontaine de la Diane
C la fontaine du Tibre
D E F G les quatre fontaines du Grand Jardin
H I les deux fontaines de la Basse Cour du
    Cheval Blanc
K La fontaine de la Cour des Offices
L source de la fontaine de fontainebleau

celle source de la fontaine
de fontainebleau a la
quelle on doit la construction
du chateau de fontaine
bleau est basse l'on y
descend par trois marches
elle est enclose par huit
panneaux formants bassin
de huit pieds de diametre en pierre
et orné ainsi il trouva peinte dans la voute
la forme de grotte l'histoire petit source trouve
parle chien bleau

voir ce que le magazin
universel page 345 dit du
palais de fontainebleau anno 1545

Plan de la fontaine de fontainebleau   voir son petit plan a L ci dessus

Henri's contemporaries and historians in the centuries that followed have always delighted in comparing him unfavorably with his predecessors, especially in the cultural field, invariably to the advantage of the Valois kings. While it cannot be denied that the Valois court was one of the most sophisticated in Europe, and that Henri excelled on the battlefield and was unrefined in his manners, at the same time Henri was not unversed in the arts, and especially in architecture, as he set about demonstrating at Fontainebleau. He turned his attention first to the old castle and its Oval Courtyard, which he opened up on its east side with a monumental gateway. While he left the buildings that overlooked the White Horse Courtyard intact, he enclosed the Jardin de la Reine (Queen's Garden) with three wings, only one of which now survives. This surviving wing houses the Galerie des Cerfs (Stags Gallery) on the ground floor, and above it the Galerie de la Reine (Queen's Gallery), now the Galerie de Diane (Diana Gallery). The garden itself was embellished with a fountain in honor of the goddess Diana. Opposite the new gateway to the Oval Courtyard, just beyond the defensive ditch excavated by Primaticcio, he built a new courtyard known as the Cour des Offices (Offices Courtyard).

Henri also gave orders for new interior decorations, commissioning painters such as the Antwerp-born Ambroise Dubois and the Parisians Toussaint Dubreuil and Martin Fréminet, and French sculptors including Mathieu Jacquet and Barthélémy Tremblay. This was the crucible from which the second School of Fontainebleau was to emerge, symbolizing—like its illustrious forebear—a measured French interpretation of Italian Mannerism. Some of the rooms in the royal apartments were given new decorative schemes. The Cabinet de la Reine (Queen's Cabinet) was hung with paintings by Ambroise Dubois narrating the story of Clorinda, while the Chambre Ovale (Oval Bedchamber), later renamed the Salon Louis XIII, was decorated with another cycle by Dubois, this time devoted to the romance of Theagenes and Chariclea.

Finally, while respecting the arrangements laid out by his predecessors, Henri was also lavish in his addition of his own monogram and portraits, fully aware as he was of the importance of celebrating this new dynasty that had succeeded in re-establishing peace within the kingdom of France. Evidence of this may be seen in the wing built by Primaticcio under Charles IX, which had not yet been decorated. Now an imposing fireplace was added, carved by Mathieu Jacquet and dedicated to Henri IV, so endowing the wing with its new name, Aile de la Belle Cheminée (Fine Fireplace Wing). The fireplace was subsequently dismantled, and its bas-relief depicting Henri IV on horseback moved to the second Salle Saint-Louis. Rooms in the newly built parts of the palace were also decorated, the Stags Gallery with images of royal palaces and forests, and the Queen's Gallery with paintings exalting the king and his military victories. Under Henri IV, Fontainebleau was the major manifestation—alongside the Louvre—of the artistic and cultural ambitions of the reign.

Louis XIII and Anne of Austria
From Restraint to Exuberance

Upon his death on May 14, 1643, Louis XIII's funeral oration proclaimed that he "did not fall prey to the pride of kings, and had no love for the century's pomp." It is a judgment borne out by the facts: Louis was no ambitious patron of the arts. Yet from childhood he had displayed a genuine interest in the arts, and particularly in Martin Fréminet's paintings for the Trinity Chapel at Fontainebleau. During his reign, moreover, he was a prolific portraitist in pastel, with Simon Vouet, First Painter to the King, and Henri Beaubrun as his drawing masters. Outside Paris, Saint-Germain-en-Laye was his favorite château, but this did not mean that he disliked Fontainebleau. During his reign, the iconic horseshoe-shaped staircase that we admire today was built by Jean Androuet de Cerceau, grandson of Jacques Androuet de Cerceau, celebrated for his album entitled *Les plus excellents bâtiments de France*. Elsewhere, the decorations of the Trinity Chapel were completed, while the Vestibule du Fer à Cheval (Horseshoe Hall) that led to the royal gallery in the chapel and the François I Gallery was embellished with new doors and paneling by Jean Gobert.

On the king's death, Anne of Austria emerged both from the shadows and from the court intrigues that had swirled around her. As queen mother and regent during the minority of Louis XIV, she proved—with the support of Cardinal Mazarin—an effective guardian of the privileges of royal power. From that point she was to occupy a position of central importance, both in politics and in the arts. At Fontainebleau she commissioned major projects, and a magnificent wooden ceiling for the Queen's Bedchamber was swiftly followed by the creation of new apartments in a block known as the Pavillon des Poêles (Stoves Pavilion). Anne of Austria had a taste for lavish profusion in decorative schemes, with rare and sumptuous embellishments combining sculpture and gilding with arabesques and grotesques in vivid colors. The furnishings of her bedchamber were hung with cloth of gold, while the chairs in her great chambers were upholstered in gold cloth patterned with silver flowers. In a decision that speaks volumes for the queen's taste, the decorations of the vestibule to the Diana Gallery were entrusted to Simon Vouet.

FACING PAGE
Portrait of Anne of Austria, Queen of France, by Peter Paul Rubens.

PAGES 72–73
The Great Salon is hung with tapestries telling the story of Alexander the Great, woven at the Gobelins manufactory after drawings by Charles Lebrun. The imposing crystal chandelier came from the Tuileries Palace.

ABOVE AND FACING PAGE

The ceiling of the Great Salon is decorated with figures representing
the planets, with Apollo in his chariot, symbol of the sun, at the center.
Carved in 1558 by Ambroise Perret, this ceiling originally adorned Henri II's
bedchamber, until it was taken down in 1660 and installed in Anne of
Austria's antechamber. The chairs with their Beauvais tapestry covers were
supplied in the early nineteenth century by Jacob-Desmalter.

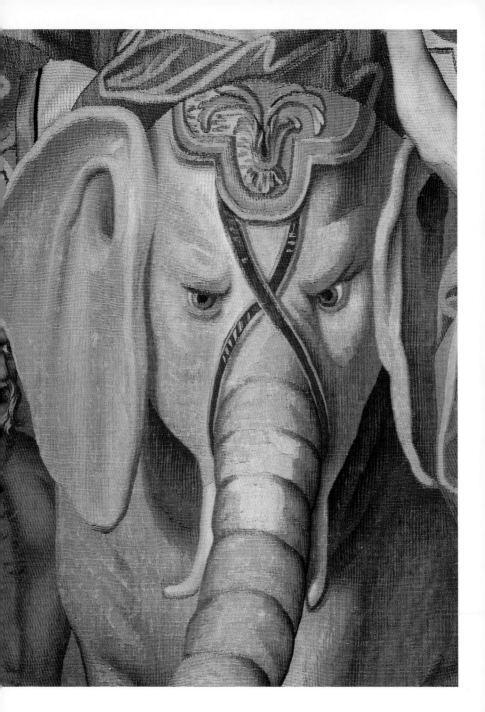

Details from the *Triumph of Mars* tapestry, Gobelins manufactory,
late seventeenth century. This is one of the eight tapestries
of the *Triumph of the Gods* cycle, after drawings by Noël Coypel;
Coypel took his inspiration in turn from a Renaissance Italian
hanging after drawings by Raphael or one of his pupils.

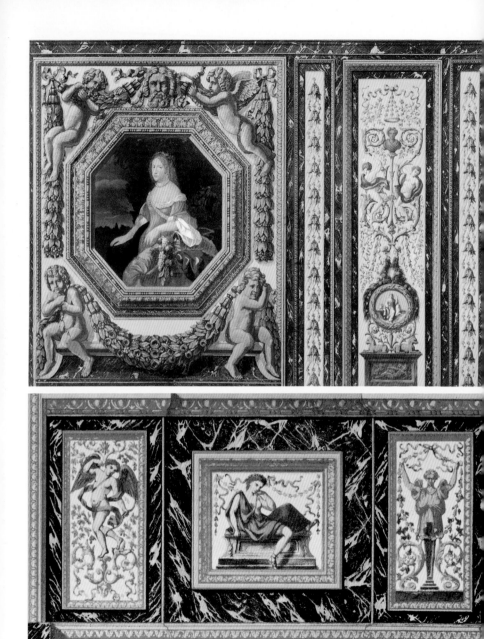

ABOVE AND FACING PAGE
Plan of the decorations for Anne of Austria's bedchamber by Rodolphe
Pfnor, with (facing page) Gilbert de Sève's portrait of Anne of Austria.
PAGES 80–81
The ceiling of Anne of Austria's bedchamber contains her double-"A"
monogram. Like the gilded and polychrome arabesques on the paneling,
it is by Charles Errard and Jean Cotelle, c. 1660.

ABOVE
Detail of the marble pavement of the Trinity
Chapel by Francesco Bordoni.

FACING PAGE
The Trinity Chapel. Built in the reigns of François I and Henri II,
it was redecorated between 1608 and 1642.

PAGES 84–85
The decoration of the chapel ceiling was commissioned by Henri IV
and designed and executed by the artist Martin Fréminet.
The central compartment depicts *Christ at the Last Judgment.*

Louis XIV at Fontainebleau:
"The Greatest Parterre in Europe"

BELOW
Aerial view of the Grand Parterre looking toward the canal, which is plied by vessels of a tonnage that appears a little over ambitious for its size.

FACING PAGE
A statue representing the Tiber, a replica of one that was destroyed during the Revolution, adorns the round pond on the Grand Parterre.

PAGES 88–89
Gondolas designed for the pleasure of the king and court float on the canal in the foreground, with a large expanse of water fed by waterfalls behind them. Above this stretches the Grand Parterre, with the palace in the right background.

Following the death of Cardinal Mazarin in March 1661, the young Louis XIV, then aged just twenty-two, decided to dispense with the office of chief minister and to embark on his personal rule. That same year, he took possession of Fontainebleau, and commanded André Le Nôtre to redesign the Grand Parterre, planted its four squares with box hedging describing the "L" of the king's monogram and the "M" of his queen, Maria Theresa. To the east of the parterre and slightly raised, Le Nôtre added a circular pool, installing at its center the statue of the Tiber that had embellished one of the garden fountains in Henri IV's time. But the allure of these new green spaces and water features was to prove short-lived, as Louis turned his attention to his favorite palace, Versailles. Nevertheless, a few new construction projects were undertaken, though chiefly for functional and administrative buildings, such as stables and lodgings for secretaries of state. But more important changes were to be made later in the king's reign.

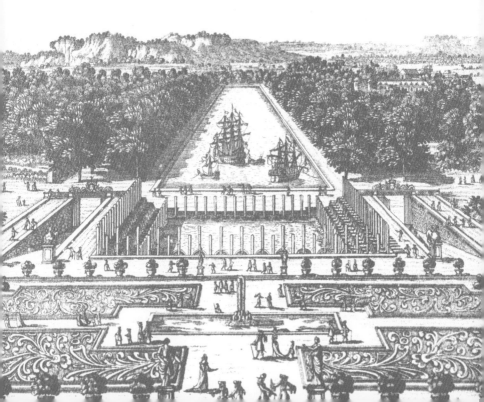

In 1685, two years after the death of Maria Theresa, Louis XIV married the Marquise de Maintenon. This secret union was morganatic, conferring none of the titles and privileges that might normally be expected by a royal bride; in 1686, however, the king ordered an apartment to be built for Madame de Maintenon above the Golden Gate at Fontainebleau. Although the decorations carried out in the summer bedchamber were altered at the start of Louis XV's reign, the original paneling in the study and the salon, originally Madame de Maintenon's bedchamber, have survived. The final years of the Sun King's reign saw a revival of major building projects at Versailles, and he himself wrote and revised several times a guide to the gardens at Versailles entitled *Manière de montrer les jardins de Versailles*. It therefore comes as no surprise to discover that he oversaw a complete redesign of some parts of the gardens at Fontainebleau, most notably enlarging the Grand Parterre to make it the largest feature of its type in the whole of Europe. All this burgeoning greenery and flourishing life was sadly belied by the waning strength of a king whose reign was drawing to its close.

Louis XV's Grand Design

Throughout his life, Louis XIV had been imbued through and through with an acute awareness of the importance of royal dignity, and so accepted without demur any inconveniences imposed by his kingly duties. Convinced that he owed his entire person to his subjects, the Sun King submitted to all the rigors of court etiquette. This temperament was not inherited by his grandson Louis XV, as the film director Thierry Binisti demonstrated in his television film, with its titular reference to the king as "the black sun." Louis XV, on the contrary, found court etiquette a cumbersome duty. To the great state apartments, where court pageantry such as the *lever du roi* and *coucher du roi* was performed daily, he therefore added a suite of private apartments. In the privacy of these more intimate rooms, he could cast off the cares and constraints of office.

At Fontainebleau, as at Versailles, Louis XV took pleasure in redesigning the apartments, and he added smaller apartments on the ground floor in the late 1730s. He was particularly attached to these rooms, and revamped their layout and decorations several times. Sadly no vestige of them now survives. The state apartments also underwent major refurbishments. The decorations in the king's apartments were updated in line with current tastes, and the layout of the rooms was also altered. Similar transformations were carried out in the queen's apartments. Nor were the royal apartments the only parts of the palace to be taken over by the king's architects, who added a new wing to the Cour des Princes (Princes' Courtyard) to house lodgings for courtiers. Most importantly, the Galerie d'Ulysse (Ulysses Gallery), a Renaissance masterpiece from the reign of Henri II, was demolished and replaced with the Louis XV Wing that still stands today, built by the architects Jacques Gabriel and his son, Ange-Jacques Gabriel, both chief architects to the king. This wing, together with the Gros Pavillon (Large Pavilion) that replaced the François I-era Stoves Pavilion, is testimony to the architectural "grand design" that envisaged a complete overhaul of the château. Circumstances, beginning with the war that exhausted the royal finances, were to ensure that this project never saw the light of day.

FACING PAGE
Doors to the Council Chamber, with decorations from the end of Louis XV's reign. Above the door is inscribed the motto *Ditat et ornat*, which may be interpreted as meaning "The king enriched and embellished this room."

PAGES 96–97
The Council Chamber as it was under the First Empire.

PAGE 98
Portrait of Maria Leszczynska with the palace of Fontainebleau in the background, attributed to Jean-Baptiste Martin the Elder (1659–1735).

PAGE 99
Ceiling of the Council Chamber, decorated with the monogram of Louis XV and paintings by François Boucher.

DITAT · · ET·ORNAT

ABOVE
Detail of a copy of *The Music Lesson* by Nicolas Lancret,
positioned as a "dessus-de-porte" (overdoor).
FACING PAGE
Interconnecting room, formerly Louis XVI's private chambers,
in the private apartments of Napoléon Bonaparte, embellished
under the Second Empire with Louis XV paneling.

Marie Antoinette:
A New Intimacy

On May 16, 1770, the wedding of Marie Antoinette, Archduchess of Austria, and Louis, Dauphin of France and grandson of Louis XV, was celebrated in the palace chapel at Versailles. It was not long before the young Marie Antoinette realized that the warmth and family-centered atmosphere that she had left behind in her childhood home in Vienna bore little relation to the glacial starchiness of life at the French court.

As the queen's bedchamber at Fontainebleau lacked any private space, Louis XVI ordered two boudoirs to be built for Marie Antoinette, the second ten years after the first. Sophisticated and intimate, these two rooms, positioned above each other, were to be the supreme examples within the confines of this immense royal palace of the refinement of the queen's private tastes.

Marie Antoinette's Boudoir Turc (Turkish Boudoir), situated above her state bedchamber, was offered to her as a gift by Louis XVI. Its decorative scheme testifies to the eclectic tastes of the time, with Turkish references in its turbans, cassolettes, perfume-burners, strings of pearls, crescent moons, and ears of corn. Its eighteenth-furniture disappeared at the Revolution; the large and sumptuous set of furniture made by Jacob for the Empress Joséphine in 1805 is currently undergoing restoration.

On the floor below, the Boudoir de la Reine or Boudoir Argent (Queen's Boudoir or Silver Boudoir), between the state bedchambers of the king and queen (the king's bedchamber was converted into Napoléon's Throne Room in 1808) was lavishly decorated in the neo-classical style by the Rousseau brothers in 1786. It was furnished with an outstanding cylinder desk and "trough" table in mother-of-pearl veneer by Riesener, which were returned to Fontainebleau in 1960. In 1786, Louis XVI, Marie Antoinette, and the court paid a visit to Fontainebleau; it was to be their last.

ABOVE
Commode made for Marie
Antoinette in 1786 by the
cabinetmaker Guillaume
Beneman, after a piece
by Joseph Stöckel.

LEFT AND FACING PAGE
Motifs of the fabric used
to decorate the Empress's
Bedchamber. The violet
Brescia marble fireplace
with its carved overmantel
was installed in the
eighteenth century for
Maria Leszczynska.
The candelabra and clock
date from the First Empire.

PAGES 106–7
Detail of the decoration
on the Beneman commode.
Interlacing plant motifs
flank a Sèvres porcelain
medallion depicting
Love as an Actor.

"These visits were delightful for their fêtes and entertainments, and for the general good humor and wit that reigned among the company there. This spirit was such that it used to be said of people who had fallen out: "If they were to find themselves together at Fontainebleau, they would be reconciled."

MADAME DE GENLIS, *DE L'ESPRIT DES ÉTIQUETTES*, ON VISITS TO THE COURT AT FONTAINEBLEAU, 1818

PAGES 108–9
The decorations of the Queen's Boudoir were designed by the architect Pierre Marie Rousseau for Marie Antoinette. The plaster high reliefs above the doors depict eight of the nine muses in pairs. In the center of the room stands the work table made in 1786 by the cabinetmaker Jean-Henri Riesener, in steel, gilt bronze, and mother-of-pearl.
ABOVE, LEFT
Portrait of Marie Antoinette by Eugénie Tripier-Lefranc after Louise-Élisabeth Vigée Le Brun.
ABOVE, RIGHT AND FACING PAGE
Details in the grotesque style from the paneling in the Queen's Boudoir.

'The day after the first performance of "Zémire et Azor," Marmontel and Grétry were presented to the queen in the gallery at Fontainebleau as she crossed it on her way to mass. Offering her compliments to Grétry on the success of the new opera, the queen told him that in the night she had had an enchanting dream of the trio of Zémire's father and sisters behind the magic mirror; then after making this compliment she continued on her way.

MADAME CAMPAN, FIRST LADY OF THE BEDCHAMBER TO MARIE ANTOINETTE, *MÉMOIRES SUR LA VIE PRIVÉE DE MARIE-ANTOINETTE*, 1823

PAGES 112–13
Created above the Queen's Bedchamber in 1777,
the Turkish Boudoir was a private space to which Marie Antoinette
could withdraw at Fontainebleau.
FACING PAGE
Emptied of its furniture at the Revolution, the boudoir was refurnished for
the Empress Joséphine, who made it her private bedchamber.

Imperial Splendor

In 1808, Napoléon turned the King's Bedchamber into his Throne Room, complete with canopy, a pair of standards topped by the imperial eagle, and a throne on a dais. The items were made by Jacob-Desmalter after designs by the architects Charles Percier and Pierre Fontaine.

PAGES 118–19

Napoléon rehearses his coronation ceremony of December 2, 1804 for the benefit of Pope Pius VII, seated in the Throne Room with Josephine on his right. Moving the figurines of the participants around on the floor, on his hands and knees, is the designer Jean-Baptiste Isabey. Engraving by Eugène Varin after Jean-Georges Vibert.

Incapable of reforming the institutions of the kingdom, Louis XVI and his ministers summoned the Estates General on May 4, 1789. There then unfolded the sequence of events that led from the Revolution to the Terror and the Consulate, via the Directory. Although it entrusted executive power to a triumvirate of consuls, the constitution that emerged from the coup d'état of 18 Brumaire, year VIII (November 9, 1799) was framed for the benefit of one man alone. Napoléon Bonaparte was determined to put an end to the Revolution. The decade since 1789 had brought about many changes at Fontainebleau. The palace furniture had been sold. Portraits of the French kings, including a magnificent portrait of Louis XIII by Philippe de Champaigne, had been burned, an act of destruction that in terms of Revolutionary vandalism—a neologism dating from the Revolution and coined by the deputy Abbé Grégoire—was a relatively minor price to pay. The palace itself remained completely undamaged, its buildings and their decorations preserved in their entirety. The installation there of the departmental École Centrale in 1796, followed in 1803 by the École Spéciale Militaire, undoubtedly played a part in ensuring this happy outcome.

Napoléon's first visit to Fontainebleau came on November 20, 1803, when the First Consul arrived to inspect the military academy housed there, before it was transferred to Saint-Cyr five years later. On May 18, 1804, the newly crowned Emperor of the French resolved to make Fontainebleau his imperial palace. One of his first decisions there was to order the demolition of the west wing of the White Horse Courtyard, running between the Ministers' Wing and the Louis XV Wing (both still standing today), and to replace it with a gateway graced with the imperial eagle. This was to be the main gateway through which visitors would henceforth enter the palace. But it was also to be the extent of major works carried out by Napoléon. Furthermore, he was so anxious to move in to the palace without more ado that he contented himself with merely refurnishing the apartments, rather than embarking on any new building projects.

ABOVE
Perched on a laurel wreath, one of the imperial eagles in the Throne Room
clutches Zeus's thunderbolt in its claws. The fabric draping the dais
is embroidered with bees, the symbol that replaced the royal fleur-de-lis.

FACING PAGE
Some of the paneling in the Throne Room had been carved
by Jacques Verberckt for Louis XV, including these doors decorated
with Hercules' club, emblem of Louis XIII.

Only the Diana Gallery, by now in an advanced state of decay, was to benefit from a complete overhaul, with Napoléon commissioning the architects Charles Percier and Pierre Fontaine to design a new gallery decorated with scenes celebrating his exploits. Percier and Fontaine also refurbished some of the palace interiors, including the emperor's private apartments.

Although Napoléon's first stays at Fontainebleau date back to 1805, he made only three official imperial visits there in the tradition of the pomp and ceremony of the royal visits of the Bourbon kings: in the fall of 1807, 1809, and 1810. On the occasion of the 1809 visit, his courtiers arrived to find that the king's former bedchamber had been transformed into a throne room, while 1810 marked the first visit to Fontainebleau by the new Empress Marie-Louise.

Napoléon's next and final visit was in April 1814. It was at Fontainebleau on April 6 that he signed the act of unconditional abdication, a painful moment made all the more bitter by his awareness of having been abandoned by so many of those whose fortunes he had made. On Wednesday April 20, he inspected the imperial guard in the White Horse Courtyard, which from that time also became known as the Cour des Adieux (Courtyard of Farewells), and made his adieus: "Soldiers of my Old Guard, I bid you farewell. For twenty years you have been my constant companions on the path to honor and victory." The ceremony immediately became famous, and gave rise to a new Napoleonic myth, to be reiterated ad infinitum by veterans of the Grande Armée nostalgic for the empire. During the Hundred Days—although he believed he was reviving all the glory of the imperial age—he simply added an extra episode (and not an especially glorious one) to this myth. Citizen Bonaparte had lost his claim to glory by his obstinate determination to continue to wage war and to refuse to make peace, on each occasion gambling double or quits on his imperial scepter. But this time he had lost for good, and there was to be no return.

'The allied powers having proclaimed that the emperor Napoléon was the sole obstacle to the re-establishment of peace in Europe, the emperor Napoléon, faithful to his oath, declares that he renounces, for himself and his children, the throne of France and Italy, and that there is no sacrifice, even of life itself, that he is not willing to make in the interests of France.

NAPOLÉON I, ACT OF ABDICATION OF APRIL 6, 1814,
WRITTEN IN HIS OWN HAND ON THE FAMOUS MAHOGANY TABLE
IN THE PALACE OF FONTAINEBLEAU

FACING PAGE
Napoléon's private drawing room, known as the Abdication Room. It was on this table, on April 6, 1814, that Napoléon signed the act of abdication.

A New King
at Fontainebleau

The kings of the restored House of Bourbon—Louis XVIII from 1814 until his death in 1824 (with the exception of the Hundred Days), and his younger brother Charles X from 1824 until he was exiled in 1830—took little interest in Fontainebleau, limiting themselves to continuing the work that Napoléon had started on the Diana Gallery. Here they took care to impose a new decorative vocabulary exalting the monarchy, the House of Bourbon, and France, and featuring figures such as Saint Louis, from whom the Bourbons were descended; Joan of Arc, who occupied a central place in nationalist sentiment; and Henri IV, the first Bourbon king.

This passion for the past, displayed here through the genre of history painting, was by no means the exclusive reserve of Louis XVIII and his brother. It permeated an

FACING PAGE
The iconographic program
of the Diana Gallery,
started under Napoléon,
was completed under
Louis XVIII. Louis-Philippe
then used the gallery as a
banqueting room. The
decorative scheme was
largely dismantled by
Napoléon III, who decided
to convert the gallery into
a library. The terrestrial
globe that stands in the
gallery vestibule was made
for Napoléon.

entire stratum of society, not only in France but throughout
Europe, as well as the world of the arts, where—in literature
as in painting and sculpture—it nurtured the new sensibility of
Romanticism. The Duc d'Orléans, who in August 1830 mounted
the throne as Louis-Philippe, was a great champion of this
notion of history, and set out to promote it by transforming
the palace of Versailles into a series of history galleries
dedicated "to all the glories of France." On his first visit to
Fontainebleau, the king of the French fell under the spell of
this ancient royal residence. Versailles might have sprung
fully formed from the genius of Louis XIV, with whom the
aging Louis-Philippe liked to compare himself, but its history
could only be traced back to the seventeenth century.
At Fontainebleau, on the other hand, he felt he was drawing
on far more distant roots. His decision was made: he would
reinvent himself as the restorer of this venerable château of
the kings of France. The intention of the approach he adopted
was not to create a perfect match between the palace rooms
on the one hand, and the history and style that was attached
to them on the other. It was more a matter of setting off what
was already there to best advantage. Today it would not be
spared by the critics. But we should not forget that it was
the restoration work carried out under Louis-Philippe that
saved Fontainebleau from decay and dereliction.

At the opposite end of the Diana Gallery stands the imposing Phidias Vase,
over 6,5 feet tall (2 metres) and made at Sèvres in 1832.

PAGES 140–41
Looking up to the ceiling of the King's Staircase, built during the reign
of Louis XV in the former bedchamber of the Duchesse d'Étampes,
mistress to François I. The wall decorations date from the Renaissance.
The ceiling painting of the *Apotheosis of Alexander the Great* was
carried out under Louis-Philippe by Abel de Pujol.

It was the first occasion since the revolution [of 1830] when I saw the king daring to remember that he was the grandson of Henri IV. This residence at Fontainebleau, so noble and aristocratic, recalled the Bourbon blood in his veins, and he developed a taste for it.

THE COMTESSE DE BOIGNE
ON LOUIS-PHILIPPE'S VISIT TO FONTAINEBLEAU, 1834

PAGE 142
Detail from the paneling in the Guardroom, carried out in a Renaissance style under Louis-Philippe.
PAGE 143
"Vase de la Renaissance," made at Sèvres in 1834 to designs by Aimé Chenavard.
FACING PAGE
Louis-Philippe decided to convert the ground-floor space under the Ballroom into a great neo-Renaissance waiting room, known then as the Salle Louis-Philippe and subsequently, after its décor, as the Columns Hall.

Napoléon III and Eugénie

BELOW
*Arrival of Their Imperial
Majesties at Fontainebleau
in 1862*, nineteenth-century
postcard.

FACING PAGE
Napoléon III, Eugénie,
and the Prince Imperial,
known as Loulou to his
parents, photograph by
Eugène Thiébault.

Napoléon III (Louis-Napoléon) did not wait for the restitution o
the empire, on December 2, 1852, to go to Fontainebleau: the
opening of the railway line from Paris to Fontainebleau, on
September 4, 1849, had already provided him with the
opportunity when he was still president of the French Republic
Two years later, the palace and former royal residence of
Fontainebleau joined his portfolio of imperial residences. But it
was not until 1857 that he and the Empress Eugénie began to
use it as their country home. The imperial couple—Napoléon II
had married Eugénie de Montijo in January 1853—were fond o
Fontainebleau, and stayed there every year. The emperor
discovered several chapters of his uncle Napoléon Bonaparte's
life there, as well as reconnecting with his own early life, for it
was at Fontainebleau that he was baptized in 1810. The Empress
meanwhile, who was strongly attached to the figure of Marie
Antoinette and had created a museum in her memory at the
Petit Trianon, took the opportunity to furnish the queen's forme
apartments with furniture of the period or in Louis XVI style.

Napoléon III was keen, moreover, to continue the
restoration work that had been started by Louis-Philippe.
Thus the Stags Gallery, built under Henri IV, was restored
to its original appearance. New building works were carried
out in the Louis XV Wing, where the emperor commanded
the architect Hector Lefuel to construct a theater, while
both he and the Empress had studies laid out for them.
Above all, the Empress Eugénie installed a Chinese museum
in the former Large Pavilion, built in the eighteenth century.
Finally, the Galerie des Fastes (Gallery of Pomp and
Splendor) displayed—in the type of dense hanging scheme
that was then the norm—paintings relating to the history
of the château. Fontainebleau's status as an imperial
residence did not stand in the way of the state apartments,
gardens and grounds being opened to the public two
afternoons a week. Long after the fall of the Second
Empire, vanquished by Prussia, and the death of her
husband, the Empress Eugénie, on a visit to Fontainebleau,
was recognized by one of the old keepers there. A month
later, Europe was plunged into the First World War.

I know of no palace that can match
Fontainebleau for such solemnities;
from the first moment it stamps them
with tremendous character; so many
kings, so many centuries have laid
their hands and left their mark
upon it that, when today history is
made there, it is made in the presence
of this great sweep of past history.

FRANÇOIS GUIZOT, STATESMAN AND HISTORIAN, IN HIS *MÉMOIRES*, 1861

ABOVE
Medallion from the cover of the official album for the Exposition Nationale Italienne
(Italian National Exhibition) of 1861, presented to Napoléon III. The year 1861 was the founding
year of the kingdom of Italy under its first king, Victor Emmanuel II.

FACING PAGE
Detail of a braid tie-back on the bed in Anne of Austria's bedchamber.

PAGES 152–53
The bedchamber of Anne of Austria, now in the Queen Mothers' Apartments,
also known as the Pope's Apartments. The Renaissance-style four-poster bed was supplied
by Fourdinois in 1860. The occasional table was a gift from Pope Pius IX to the Prince Imperial,
his godson. The walls are hung with tapestries from the *Triumph of the Gods* cycle,
woven after drawings by Noël Coypel in the late seventeenth century.

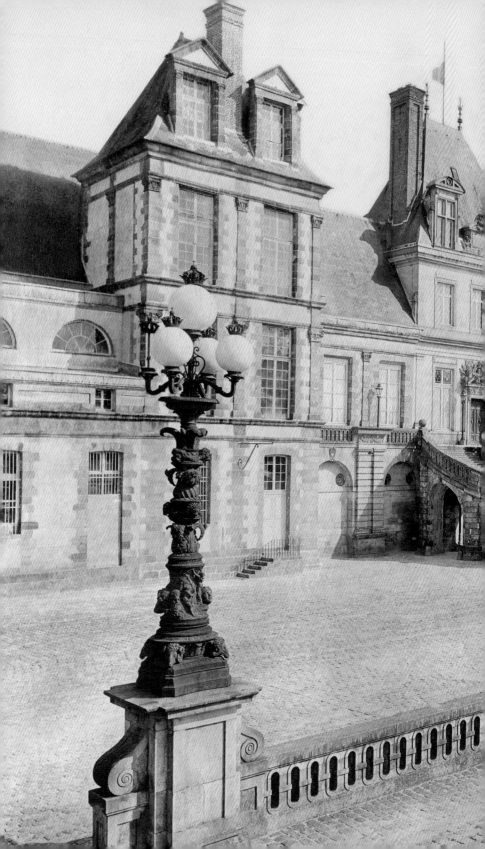

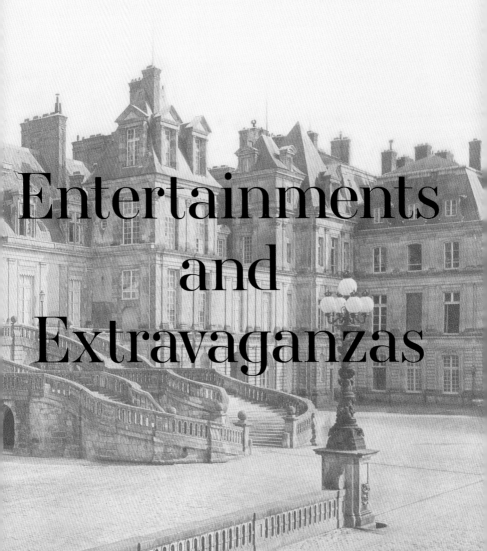

Entertainments
and
Extravaganzas

Fontainebleau:
A Setting for Diplomacy

According to the archives, Thomas Becket, Archbishop of Canterbury, was the first distinguished guest to be received at Fontainebleau, in 1169, when he was invited by Louis VII to consecrate the new chapel. In 1325, Philippe le Bel's daughter Isabella—dubbed the "She-Wolf of France" by Maurice Druon in his famous novels *Les rois maudits* (*The Accursed Kings*)—was the guest at Fontainebleau of her brother Charles IV. Married to the English king Edward II, she had crossed the Channel in a bid to ease the tensions between the two kingdoms. Plagued as she was by the hostility that existed between herself and Edward's favorite and adviser Hugh Despenser, she is also believed to have sought her brother's support in toppling Despenser and deposing Edward.

Two centuries later, in 1539, the Holy Roman Emperor Charles V was François I's guest at Fontainebleau from December 24 to 30. His arrival was celebrated with tournaments held outside the Golden Gate, then the main entrance to the château. Over a century later, from October 1657 to February 1658 it was the turn of Queen Christina to stay at Fontainebleau after abdicating the throne of Sweden. Suspecting the Marchese Monaldeschi, her master of the horse, of treachery, she had him murdered in the Stags Gallery, which cast a certain chill over her relations with the French court. In July 1664, Louis XIV received a papal legate who had come to Fontainebleau to present him with the apologies of Pope Alexander VII, following an altercation in Rome between the pontiff's Corsican Guard and the French servants and guards of the French ambassador. Subsequently, the Sun King devoted himself to high politics, and thus it was that, during the crisis over the Spanish succession following the death of Charles II, he took important advice on several occasions in the apartments of Madame de Maintenon. After considerable hesitation he accepted the terms of Charles's will, so dragging his kingdom into yet another war—though admittedly this one would have been more difficult to avoid than the two preceding ones.

PAGES 154–55
Nineteenth-century photograph of the horseshoe staircase and balustrade.

FACING PAGE
The Reception of the Siamese Ambassadors by Napoléon III in the Ballroom at the Palace of Fontainebleau, June 27, 1861 by Jean-Léon Gérôme (detail). To the right of the imperial couple sits the young Prince Imperial.

MARIAGE DE LOUIS
XV·CELEBRE LE V SEPT
1725

Within the image, the following labels appear:

Chateau Royal de Fontainebleau

entrée du Château

tronpette du Roy

Carosse de M. d'Orleans

Officier de M. le Duc d…

Gendarmes

Chevaux legèr

Carosse de la Reine

Mousquetaires

la C. de Mauly dans le Carosse de la reine

Valet de … de la … Reine

In the nineteenth century, Fontainebleau continued to welcome prestigious visitors, not all of whom came willingly. Napoléon had Pope Pius VII put under house arrest there for nineteen months from June 1812, as punishment for defying the economic blockade on his enemies. In June 1861, Napoléon III and Eugénie received an embassy from the King of Siam, Rama IV Mongkut, in the Ballroom, a scene famously depicted by Jean-Léon Gérôme in a painting that now hangs at Versailles. The gifts presented to the imperial couple have stayed at Fontainebleau, where some of them are now displayed in the Empress's Chinese museum.

In an age when marriages played an essential part in affairs of state, several weddings of significance were celebrated at Fontainebleau. On September 5, 1725, the thorny matter of who should be the bride of Louis XV was settled with his marriage to Marie Leszczynska, daughter of the deposed King of Poland, whose short-lived reign had lasted from 1704 until 1709. In preparation for this event, a new theater was built in the Fine Fireplace Wing, which involved demolishing the splendid fireplace built under Henri IV from which the building took its name. On their wedding day, two Molière plays—*Amphitryon* and *Le médecin malgré lui* (*A Doctor in Spite of Himself*)—were performed in the bridal couple's honor. The great playwright of the Grand Siècle was still in vogue, to the great delight of the court. On May 30, 1837, after a century featuring a series of regime changes, the ceremonies surrounding the nuptials of Louis-Philippe's eldest son, the Duc d'Orléans, and Princess Helene of Mecklenburg-Schwerin also took place at Fontainebleau.

By the end of the century the Third Republic was receiving state visitors there, with President Félix Faure welcoming Leopold II, king of the Belgians, in 1895. This tradition continued into the second half of the twentieth century. In June 1984, François Mitterrand hosted a meeting of the European Council, comprising the heads of state of every EEC member state, at Fontainebleau. Since then, the palace has focused on its cultural role, and especially on admitting the public as visitors. All the same, lying as it does in direct descent from François I's vision of it, Fontainebleau remains not only a compelling symbol, but also—as the patrons of all nationalities who have so generously supported and financed renovation and restoration projects over the years have so well understood—a prestigious ambassador for the art and history of France.

Celebrations and Entertainments

In 1682, Louis XIV gave the hitherto peripatetic French court a permanent home at Versailles. From September to November every year, nonetheless, the king stayed at Fontainebleau, where he allowed the rigorous etiquette that was the rule at Versailles to be slightly relaxed. As summer drew to a close every year, there would be only one subject of conversation at court: the "trip to Fontainebleau," a tradition that was to persist until the Revolution.

In the eighteenth century, under Louis XV and Louis XVI, Fontainebleau became the setting for intense programs of live performances. The performances given at the palace signaled the opening of the court entertainment season, which would run through to Easter of the following year. French and Italian theater troupes, together with the musicians of the Académie Royale de Musique, would mount glittering productions chosen from a repertoire of operas, ballets, and plays. Among the most successful productions in the late eighteenth century were operas such as Jean-Philippe Rameau's *Dardanus* and *Anacréon* and Jean-Jacques Rousseau's *Le devin de village* (The Village Soothsayer), as well as comic operas such as *Zémire et Azor* and *Richard Cœur-de-lion* by André-Modeste Grétry, both of which were particular favorites of Marie Antoinette.

Louis XV cared little for the theater, and was happy to leave the programming to his mistresses, Madame de Pompadour, and later Madame du Barry. Louis XVI was equally unenthusiastic initially, but in the end—under the influence of Marie Antoinette—became a theater-goer. Sixty years later, Napoléon III and Eugénie continued this program of entertainments at Fontainebleau. On Mondays, Wednesdays, and Saturdays, the imperial couple and

ABOVE
Plan of the old theater, created in 1725
for the marriage of Louis XV in the Fine Fireplace Wing.
It burned down in 1856.

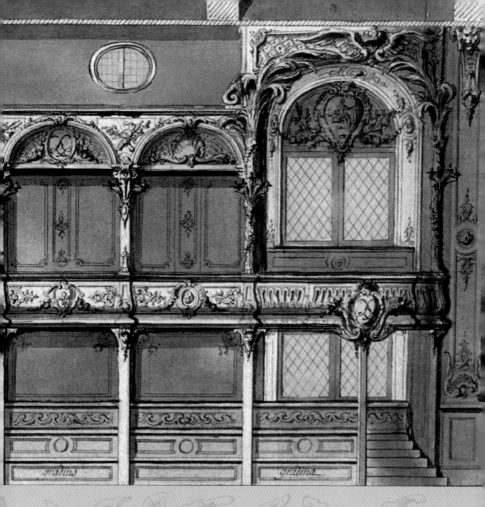

"The entire court is entranced by your piece [The Village Soothsayer]: the king, who as you know dislikes music, sings your melodies all day long, in a voice that is more off-key than the worst in his kingdom, and is demanding another performance in a week's time.

PIERRE DE JÉLYOTTE TO JEAN-JACQUES ROUSSEAU, 1752

ABOVE
Design for a nymph's costume for *Sylvie*, an opera in three acts
performed at Fontainebleau in 1765.

FACING PAGE
In 1853, Napoléon III decided to build a new theater in the Louis XV Wing:
section of the design for the imperial box.

PAGES 168–69
In 2014, the Imperial Theater, inaugurated by Napoléon III and Eugénie and closed for the last 150 years, was opened to the public once more.

ABOVE
Invitations to a performance at the Imperial Theater under Napoléon III and Eugénie.

FACING PAGE
The imperial foyer.

PAGES 172–73
View from the stage of the Imperial Theater. The ceiling is decorated with an *Allegory of Music and Poetry* by André Charles Voillemot.

the court would watch performances by the actors of the Comédie-Française, while on Sundays concerts would be given in the state apartments. Napoléon III decided to replace the old theater, built in 1725 and now dated, with a new one, built in 1853–56 by Hector Lefuel. In a stroke of synchronicity, the old theater burned down on the very night that the new one opened. In a part of the Louis XV Wing that had never been completed, Lefuel built a state-of-the-art 400-seat theater equipped with all the latest features: vestibules, staircases, salons, a stage and under-stage area, as well as facilities for the actors, musicians, and stagehands. Lefuel designed an elliptical auditorium rising through four levels: stalls, a lower circle with the imperial box, an upper circle, and boxes with grilles up in the gods. The design was directly inspired by Marie Antoinette's Little Theater at Versailles—a decision that was by no means coincidental, given the Empress Eugénie's passionate interest in the martyr queen. Opened in May 1857, the theater was used for a mere fifteen or so performances.

In 1834, Louis-Philippe and his queen, Maria Amalia, had revived the famous "trip to Fontainebleau" that had been so dear to the courts of Louis XV and Louis XVI. Napoléon III and Eugénie followed suit, making Fontainebleau their country residence every summer. From 1852 to 1870, the imperial couple would invite groups of forty to fifty guests to the palace to share their daily lives. Regular visitors on their guest list, which changed over on a weekly basis, included Prosper Mérimée, inspector of historic monuments, academician, and member of Eugénie's inner circle, and Princess Pauline Metternich, wife of the Austrian ambassador to Paris and a noted wit who famously quipped, "I'm not pretty; I'm worse." Each guest was allotted his or her own furnished apartment, and now once again court etiquette was markedly more relaxed at Fontainebleau than in Paris. The fall of the empire in 1870, following Napoléon III's defeat at Sedan by the Prussian king and German princes, put an end to these imperial entertainments.

Water, Water Everywhere

Fontainebleau takes its name from the freshwater spring around which the original settlement grew up. The gently sloping site prevented the waters of the little River Changis from flowing away properly, while the sandy soil favored the formation of springs. The lake over which the Cour de la Fontaine (Fountain Courtyard) looks was already a feature in the Middle Ages, and in order to drain this damp, marshy spot to make a garden, François I ordered the construction of a network of small canals, which would form part of a space intended for games, strolling, and taking the air. Following a period of neglect during the Wars of Religion (1562–98), Henri IV, who was greatly attached to Fontainebleau, embarked on a building program featuring not only buildings but also gardens and water features. Major fountains embellished with sculptures were installed in the gardens. A statue of Diana adorned the Queen's Garden, while the Grand Parterre gained a figure of the Tiber. Most important of all, the first Bourbon king decided to create a vast canal nearly 3940 feet long (1,200 meters), which became the spectacular setting for grand occasions. For the celebrations honoring the marriage of Louis XV and Marie Leszczynska, on September 5, 1725, a trained cormorant gave a display of fishing in the canal. The following day a different spectacle awaited the court, as music rose as if by magic from the unruffled waters (in fact from two gondolas). The young queen, who had

forsaken the cumbersome carriages of the previous reign for an open barouche, was delighted.

The Carp Pond overlooked by the Fountain Courtyard was so large that it was an open invitation to take to the water. During François I's reign, courtiers could board a flotilla of small boats from a covered landing stage on a level with the courtyard. The Carp Pond also made a picturesque backdrop to some spirited open-air performances. In July 1661, a stage was built beside the lake for a performance of the Ballets des Saisons with music by Jean-Baptiste Lully. The dancers were Louis XIV and some of his courtiers. Under Louis XIII, a pavilion was built in the middle of the pond, where, according to *Le Trésor des merveilles de la maison royale de Fontainebleau* (The Royal House of Fontainebleau's Treasure Trove of Marvels), courtiers could enjoy "the cool air in summer and relax in the midst of the waters." In 1662, this was replaced by another pavilion, octagonal in plan. At the end of Louis XIV's reign, Pierre Denis Martin's *View of the Château and Gardens at Fontainebleau after the Improvements of 1713* depicted a golden gondola—doubtless the king's pleasure craft—on the pond. The pavilion was restored under Napoléon Bonaparte, who liked to take Marie-Louise (whose pregnancy had been announced in July 1810) out for trips on the pond in a prettily decorated gondola, a gift from the city of Nantes. Under the Second Empire, Empress Eugénie fitted out the pavilion as a comfortable spot for excursions for the imperial couple's weekly guests.

In the late nineteenth century, postcards were put on sale showing the miniature frigate built for the Prince Imperial, only son of Napoléon III and Eugénie. Drifting aimlessly on the still waters of the Carp Pond, the vessel seems to recall with a hint of nostalgia the regime that had been succeeded by the Third Republic after the defeat at Sedan.

After luncheon, we went down into the garden and amused ourselves with boating on the pond, where boats of every variety, and even a Venetian gondola with genuine Venetian gondolier, were put at the guests' disposal.

PRINCESS METTERNICH, 1860—1869

Imperial
Memories

BELOW

Detail of an overdoor
in the Yellow Salon in
the Empress's private
apartments.

FACING PAGE

Egyptian figure adorning
one of the posts of the
Emperor's bed installed
in the bedchamber of his
private apartments.

During its long history, Fontainebleau has played host to
two emperors. Under the First Empire, Napoléon Bonaparte
stayed there initially with Josephine, and after their
divorce in December 1809, with Marie-Louise. It was
at Fontainebleau, on April 6, 1814, that he signed his
abdication. Under the Second Empire, Napoléon III and
the Empress Eugénie chose Fontainebleau as their country
home, entertaining their guests there every summer
from 1857—and so leaving more of a mark on the place
than their great ancestor Napoléon Bonaparte.

ABOVE AND FACING PAGE
The Emperor's Library, in the private imperial apartments.
The bookcases were brought from the château of Saint-Cloud.
The staircase leads up to the Diana Gallery.

The Empress's Bedchamber, in her private apartments.
ABOVE
"Somno," in mahogany, bronze, and green marble, by François-Honoré-Georges
Jacob-Desmalter. Empress's Bedchamber, private apartments.
FACING PAGE
Giltwood sofa covered in green velvet, by Pierre-Gaston Brion.
Second room in the Emperor's Study, private apartments.

The Chinese Museum

Among the palace rooms laid out by Napoléon III and Eugénie, the Empress's Chinese museum has been preserved just as it was in the imperial couple's time. Eugénie wanted to bring together and to display under one roof her collections of art and objects from the Far East, which came from the imperial wardrobe, from acquisitions made by the imperial couple, from the sacking of the Summer Palace in Peking (Beijing) by a Franco-British expeditionary force in 1860, and from diplomatic gifts from the Siamese embassy received at Fontainebleau in 1861. Eugénie decided to install her museum on the ground floor of the Large Pavilion built under Louis XV, in an enfilade of rooms looking out over the Carp Pond and the garden à l'anglaise, a haven of peace, bathed in sunlight and set among the cool greenery of the gardens. The Empress personally directed the conversion of the rooms that were to form her museum, which was opened in the presence of a select gathering on June 14, 1863. Following the fall of the Second Empire in 1870, the contents of the museum remained the same but the displays were altered. It was only in the early 1990s, after works lasting seven years, that the museum was reopened with its collections displayed as the Empress intended. The palace of Fontainebleau takes pleasure in fostering the memory of its former inhabitants, who did so much to maintain and embellish it.

We went into the Chinese
drawing room to take tea.
The curiosities there are
magnificent: pagodas of gold
and enamel, huge idols,
and gigantic vases glittering
in the light of chandeliers
and candelabras.

OCTAVE FEUILLET TO HIS WIFE, 1863

PAGES 198–99
The New Chinese Museum of Her Imperial Majesty,
engraving published in *Le Monde illustré* in 1863.
FACING PAGE
Candelabra by Ferdinand Barbedienne made from a large vase cornet
in cloisonné enamel, one of the five offering vessels of the traditional ritual
wugong that would be placed before altar tables in temples.
ABOVE
One of the pair of dragons flanking the Buddhist stupa.

Painted glass lantern
in the Chinese museum, nineteenth century.
Gilt bronze and cloisonné enamel incense
burner, Qianlong period.

Hunting:
The Sport of Kings

From the Middle Ages until the Revolution, French society was founded on the notion of privilege, and on the inequalities that shored it up. One such privilege was hunting, an activity that was the exclusive preserve of the aristocracy, and from which the lower orders—merchants, artisans, and peasants—were banned. As head of the aristocracy and of Ancien Régime society, the king was viewed as the huntsman par excellence, and hunting as a royal pastime. The attractions of the royal residences depended largely on the hunting forests and the variety and quantity of game they could offer. When the Capetian kings went to Fontainebleau in the twelfth and thirteenth centuries, they went there to hunt. It was at Fontainebleau, moreover, that Philippe le Bel died in 1314, following an accident while out hunting stags in the dense forests that surrounded the château.

BELOW
Misse and Turlu, two of Louis XV's greyhounds, by Jean-Baptiste Oudry.
FACING PAGE
Death of the Stag in the Ponds at Saint-Jean-aux-Bois (detail) by Jean-Baptiste Oudry, eighteenth century.

Two centuries later, on his return from captivity in Madrid, François I decided to leave the Loire Valley for the Île-de-France. When he was not in Paris, his favorite residence was Fontainebleau, which was fêted for its forests teeming with game and for the prolonged hunting parties in which he was at leisure to indulge, as specified in a letter patent signed by him in 1529: "considering that we intend and are decided hereafter to make it our principal residence for the pleasure that we find in the said place and in hunting the red and black game in the forest of Bierre and its environs."

Thus from the Middle Ages a custom was established that was to be passed down from one dynasty to the next. After the Valois, the Bourbons carried on the custom of hunting at Fontainebleau, and even decorated some of the palace rooms according to a hunting theme, including the Stags Gallery, with its depictions of royal residences and forests, interspersed with mounted stags' heads (forty-two of them by 1642). At the end of Louis XV's reign, the gallery was converted into apartments for the king's daughters. Of all the Bourbon kings, he was nevertheless unrivaled in his passion for hunting, as evidenced in the famous set of drawings by Jean-Baptiste Oudry depicting *The Royal Hunts of Louis XV*, intended for the Gobelins tapestry workshops. In 1835, Louis-Philippe commanded that these paintings be set into the walls of the princes' apartments, known ever since as the Appartements des Chasses (Hunting Apartments). In 1860, Napoléon III, following in his uncle's footsteps and himself a keen huntsman, set out to restore the Stags Gallery to its original appearance. The royal and imperial hunting horns may have fallen silent, but the palace keeps their memory alive.

"Fontainebleau, son château et sa forêt"

Western European societies in the second half of the nineteenth century saw the growth of what we would now call the leisure industry, and prominent among the new leisure activities of the privileged few was tourism. The rise of tourism coincided with the golden age of the lithographic printing process, which meant images could be reproduced on a large scale, and in color as well as monochrome. So the advertising poster was born, and the walls of towns and cities became plastered with a colorful array of printed posters.

Served as it was by a railway line opened by the future Napoléon III in 1849, Fontainebleau, with its palace and forest, rapidly became a popular tourist spot. Ever-increasing numbers of posters advertised its attractions: one printed in 1891 was entitled "Fontainebleau, son château et sa forêt," adding—as if to dismiss any lingering hesitation—"Fontainebleau, à 1 heure de Paris" ("an hour from Paris").

BELOW
Travel label from the Grand Hôtel de l'Aigle Noir at Fontainebleau.

FACING PAGE
Statue of Flora in the English Garden.

PAGES 212–13
The English Garden.

The advertising slogans hit their target and visitors thronged to its delights, attracted by images of the hunt, now open to all and not just the elite; of the Courtyard of Farewells, where Napoléon bade goodbye to the Old Guard on April 20, 1814; the pavilion in the middle of the Carp Pond; and above all the forest, with its "Charlemagne" oak planted in 1802. Crisscrossed by a large network of paths and walks, the forest offered a variety of itineraries suitable for both seasoned walkers and inexperienced newcomers. While the royal forest, corresponding to the Forêt de Bierre, covered 42 acres (17,000 hectares), today the palace is surrounded by over 49 acres (20,000 hectares) of woodland. Efforts to preserve some of the species that grow there date back to long before the ecological concerns of today. In 1861, the first "artistic reserve"—a precursor of nature reserves—was created, covering some thousand hectares of forest. In more recent years, cycling and mountain-biking, climbing and motorcycle trails have taken the place of horseracing, hunting to hounds, golf, and other traditionally fashionable pursuits. Fashions may change, but the former royal palace and its forest are more popular with visitors than ever.

The Americans' Arrival

In the summer of 1923, the financier and philanthropist John D. Rockefeller, Jr. came to France, his first visit since 1906. "Impressed once again by the beauty of her art, the magnificence of her architecture and the splendors of her gardens," he was deeply saddened by the state of dereliction in which he found many of the country's great monuments. In 1924, he wrote to the head of the French government proposing that he should contribute to the restoration of three monuments that he believed formed "part of the heritage of all nations." He allotted a considerable sum to the rebuilding of the roof of Reims Cathedral, which had been destroyed by bombing during the First World War; to the restoration of the buildings, fountains, and gardens at Versailles; and to urgent repairs to the palace and gardens at Fontainebleau. Thanks to the generosity of this wealthy and cultivated patron, Fontainebleau—like France before it—was to be saved by the intervention of America.

The Fine Fireplace Wing, restored thanks to the patronage
of John D. Rockefeller, Jr. from 1924 to 1931.
John D. Rockefeller, Jr. with his father, John D. Rockefeller, in 1915.

A few years earlier, the Americans had already invaded the palace. In 1921, the German-born American composer Walter Damrosch, conductor of the New York Symphony Orchestra, and the French conductor Francis Casadesus set up the American Conservatory (Conservatoire américain de Fontainebleau), under the direction of Casadesus and the organist and composer Charles-Marie Widor. Every year, over 150 students came to study for a period of three months, and soon the conservatory gained an international reputation, notably thanks to the talent of the organist, pianist, and conductor Nadia Boulanger, musical director from 1948 until her death in 1979. In 1923, the École des Beaux-Arts opened with a similar mission in the fields of painting, sculpture, and architecture, though it soon focused exclusively on architecture.

In the period after the Second World War, Fontainebleau's American links were strengthened yet further. In 1949, Belgium, France, Luxembourg, the Netherlands, and the United Kingdom signed the North Atlantic Treaty with Canada and the United States, so forming the NATO alliance, with the aim of defending western Europe against any potential Soviet threat. American military bases were established in the member countries, and Fontainebleau hosted the general staff of Allied Forces in Central Europe. In 1967, France partially withdrew from NATO, and the Americans withdrew from Fontainebleau: "O say does that star-spangled banner yet wave, O'er the land of the free and the home of the brave?"

FONTAINEBLEAU
SCHOOL OF FINE ARTS
FOR AMERICAN STUDENTS
SESSION MCMXXIV

EXECUTIVE DIRECTOR
Suzanne Tise-Isoré
Style & Design Collection

EDITORIAL COORDINATION
Inès Ferrand

GRAPHIC DESIGN
Bernard Lagacé
Assisted by Jean-Rémi Agin

TRANSLATED FROM THE FRENCH BY
Barbara Mellor

COPYEDITING
Sarah Kane

PROOFREADING
Michael Thomas

PRODUCTION
Élodie Conjat

COLOR SEPARATION
Les Artisans du Regard, Paris

PRINTED BY
Tien Wah Press, Malaysia

With the participation of the Public
Establishment of the Château de Fontainebleau
Étienne Chilot, publishing manager

Simultaneously published in French
as *Un jour à Fontainebleau*
© Flammarion, S.A., Paris, 2015

English-language edition
© Flammarion, S.A., Paris, 2015

Flammarion S.A.
87, quai Panhard et Levassor
75647 Paris Cedex 13
editions.flammarion.com
styleetdesign-flammarion.com

Dépôt légal: 10/2015
15 16 17 3 2 1
ISBN: 978-2-08-020254-3

Photographic Credits

All photographs in this book were taken by Eric Sander with the exception of the following:

Acknowledgments

Éditions Flammarion wishes to thank Jean-François Hebert,
president of the Château de Fontainebleau,
for his trust and his valuable help.
We are grateful to Étienne Chilot, Vincent Cochet,
Patricia Da Costa, Hubert Dagry, Vincent Droguet,
Éric Grebille, Alexis de Kermel, Patricia Kalensky,
Guillaume Larbi, Irina Metzl, and Sarah Paronetto.
We are very thankful to Marie-Dominique Ehlinger
for opening the precious archives of the Bibliothèque
Municipale de la ville de Fontainebleau to us.